THE GOLDEN BOO

OPORTO
AND NORTHERN PORTUGAL

Text by
JÚLIO L. COUTO
Photographs by
JEAN CHARLES PINHEIRA

© Copyright by CASA EDITRICE BONECHI
Via Cairoli, 18/b Firenze - Italia - Tel.+39 055576841 - Fax +39 0555000766
E-mail: bonechi@bonechi.it - Internet: www.bonechi.it

Printed in Italy by Centro Stampa Editoriale Bonechi.

Photographs from the Archives of Casa Editrice Bonechi taken by Jean Charles Pinheira.

* * *

A panoramic view.

INTRODUCTION

The region north of the Douro River covers part of the medieval territory of Antre Douro and Minho and the area beyond Marão. This is Northern Portugal, where the Atlantic waters are colder and where vessels have recently started to ply the great waterway of the Douro once more. The days of boats such as the rabelos, rabões and valboeiros are past, while their modern-day counterparts on the left bank of the Douro are basically for the benefit of the tourists, an added attraction to the traditional cellars of the famous port wine industry before which they lie at anchor.

Portugal and her second largest and busiest city take their names from the Roman Portus Calle, on the Douro estuary. This area corresponded to the County of Portucale which was presented to Count Henrique of Burgundy, on his marriage to Tareja, the illegitimate daughter of King Afonso IV of León and Castille. But intrigue, to which the Gallician Count of Trava and Bishop Gelmires were no strangers, was

rife. When Count Henrique died, his son Infante D. Afonso, became lord of these lands and was soon carried away with a desire for independence and a kingdom of his own. Duly proclaimed king in 1128 by his followers, Afonso Henriques succeeded in vanquishing the hosts of Leon and Castille, and made ready to move south, overpowering the Arabs who sought vainly to stand in his way.

In this part of the peninsula, the conquered were not treated as in the rest of Europe at that time. Provided the laws of the day were observed and the established taxes paid, the defeated, Arabs, Christians or Jews alike, were left alone to live their lives and even to practice their religions. The Inquisition had little influence in Northern Portugal — a single auto-da-fé in Oporto — although the Jews went so far as to invent the alheira of Tras-os-Montes — a sausage of calf gut stuffed with poultry and bread — which was hung in the smokehouse like the Christian pork sausages. And,

Vine terraces on the Douro.

Hinterland and the Douro River.

let it be added, that "it deceived only those who wished to be deceived". Descendants of the marranos, Jews who had "officially" converted, are still to be found today and in Oporto there is a fine synagogue, as in many other Portuguese cities, while Lisbon's mosque is a living example of the tolerant harmony of life in Portugal. This broad-minded attitude is apparent throughout the North, in the densely populated province of Minho with its red-tiled cottages of granite or in wild Trás-os-Montes and its traditional thatched slate houses. The way in which manor houses and castles are set among modern dwellings, which are often in extremely bad taste, keeps alive the genuine character and typical features of these provinces.

Throughout the north of Portugal, outside the ancient towns — and sometimes even within them — the pace of life is governed by the tranquility of people in harmony with their surroundings, at home with their customs and traditions, enlivened now and again by the feast days of the patron saint of their respective village. And then you may witness the gaiety of the emigrants whose pleasure in seeing their families is so much more keenly felt as they help prepare the celebrations in honour of "their" saint. It is a celebration within a celebration. These few days seem to compensate for the time spent working far from home in foreign lands, whether one year or many. The festivities centre around the procession with baldachins and portable platforms carried waist or shoulder high by the faithful, with the obligatory white-winged cherubs reflected in the rapt eyes of the family members. And it is a pleasure that will last through yet another year of renewed toil and yearning, resolutely forgotten for the moment, interspersed with the pleasure of offering a warm embrace to visitors, for everybody is welcome...

4

Two views of the city.

OPORTO

From earliest days, the inhabitants of Portucale, who lived on the steep slopes that climbed from the Douro up to the Cividade peak and dropped down on the other side to the Rio da Vila, submitted to the attraction of the river at their feet, reminding them that only work could open the doors which, in those days, were normally opened only to those with family connections. And so they laboured, zealously protective of the privileges they had been granted — and of which they had so often been forcibly deprived — and of their natural pride as free men, pride born of the sweat that poured down their bodies as they returned to the comfort of home, with the satisfaction of a duty fulfilled and in the security of a few more coins saved against a rainy day.

As masters of their own fate, they never forgot the river which had been their cradle and they turned its banks into ship yards and they turned the trees into keels and ribs, some trunks even serving for the masts and rigging on the ships journeying to the Basque Country, the Channel, Flanders or Morocco, to the Barbary states, Venice and Genoa. King Joaõ I had

A view of the city from Vila Nova de Gaia.

The Ribeira *district.*

A view of the city.

honoured himself and the city by marrying his English wife here in his home by the **Alfândega Velha***, and the populace had lent him their support both financially and with fighting men. In 1415 when his son, D. Duarte, came to ask their help in organizing a fleet to carry him, with his brothers and his father, to Ceuta they promptly responded. Victory would earn them the right to become armed knights, and so they redoubled their efforts in the production of keels, rigging, masts and sails, to such an extent that the chronicler Azurara stated that: "the traffic between those banks was such that neither by day nor by night was it still". And everything was made ready in time. All that was wanting were sea biscuits and meat to feed the crews. And so the women kneaded dough and the youths filled*

barrels with water (and others with vinho fino*), and the men slaughtered and salted the meat and the fleet set sail loaded with the necessary provisions.*
Oporto was left with nothing but offal. But, as the poet Rodrigues Canedo wrote:

"Por isso te hei-de cantar
heróico povo, altaneiro,
que, para ajudar o Infante
a abrir o mar, triunfante,
até de comer deixaste,
mas, para sempre ganhaste
a honra de ser tripeiro"

"For this I serenade you, proud, heroic people, who, to help the Infante to set sail, triumphantly, you went even without food,
but won for yourselves the title of *tripeiro* (offal eater)"

10

A view of the city and the Igreja dos Congregados *in the foreground;* Rua dos Clérigos *in downtown Oporto.*

The Almeida Garrett *square and the* Igreja dos Congregados.

THE BRIDGES

Until recently, this was the city of three bridges. Today it has four, and a fifth is contemplated.

The first was a pontoon bridge, which was responsible for a major accident at the time of the French invasion under General Soult, Duke of Dalmatia, in March 1809. The bridge was laid over boats lying side by side and served to carry people and goods. When the French arrived and the defenders led by the Bishop António de Castro retreated, the bridge gave way and the first French cavalry to reach the **Ribeira** (river bank) was greeted by the sight of countless corpses bobbing in the water. A statue by Teixeira Lopes (senior) is set in the Ribeira wall to this day. Everybody knows the "*Alminhas da Ponte*" — Souls of the Bridge —, before which the local people still place flowers and candles.

Next came the suspension bridge. The supports are still visible, though more clearly on the Oporto bank than on the Gaia side. A little over a century ago, Gustave Eiffel came to Oporto and, using the "Meccano" system with which we all played as children, built a bridge consisting of 640 tons of steel, measuring 350 metres in length, its carriageway suspended 60 metres above the mean water level of the river below.

The bridge was given the name of **Dona Maria** (wife

Views of the Dom Luis *bridge.*

of King Luiz I), and was inaugurated on 1 November, 1877, in the presence of the royal couple and the event was marked by the crossing of the first train coming into Oporto from the south.

Eiffel's disciple and colleague in the construction of this bridge, Teófilo Seyring, decided to design another bridge, to be dedicated to **Dom Luíz I**, based on Eiffel's design and incorporating two carriageways for pedestrians and vehicles. The bridge is 392 metres long and 8 metres wide, the arch spans 442 metres, and the whole required 3,000 tons of iron. The bridge was inaugurated on October 31, 1886.

Then the **Ponte da Arrábida** was begun in 1960. A pleasant design by the engineer Edgar Cardoso, it was inaugurated on 22 June, 1963. It consists of a concrete carriageway, supported by an arch with a 500 metre span, at the time thought to be impossible, suspended 70 metres above the level of the river waters and standing on 150,000 tons of concrete. Still another bridge, once more designed by Edgar Cardoso, was inaugurated on 24 June, 1991. This "crazy" work of engineering was also severely criticized but it cannot be denied that it is at once elegant and serviceable, carrying all the trains running between Oporto and the South.

Now a new bridge is contemplated, this time further upstream, for motor vehicles and pedestrians. We hope that it lives up to the standard of the previous bridges.

The harbour of the Ribeira *district.*

RIBEIRA

Ribeira and its market are a world apart in the special world of Oporto. The arches are all part of the so-called *fernandina* wall, which was not completed until the XIV century, during the reign of King Fernando I. The wharf was designed by the fifteenth century court architect, António da Costa who immediately eliminated one of the gates in the wall facing the river, the *Postigo do Carvão* — Coal Hatch. Later, the great promoters of the architectural revolution in the Oporto of the XVIII century, the Almadas (father and son) demolished almost the entire city wall and, in the process, they took every opportunity to flatter crown prince João and the entire court over which the infamous *Marquês de Pombal* presided. They covered over the **Rio da Vila**, which still flows beneath the street named **Rua S. João** and enters the Douro here in the **Ribeira**. They broadened the **Praça da Ribeira**, and gave it an enormous fountain, also dedicated to São João, bearing the royal coat of arms and a niche which is still waiting for the statue that it was supposed to contain. The design of the whole core of the **Praça da Ribeira** was handed over to an Englishman by the name of Whitehead — architect of the pleasing **Feitoria Inglesa**, immediately above the **Rua de São João** — who decided to give the square an English atmosphere. Fortunately he got no further than the left side.

Six or seven years ago, the local council commissioned

the great painter and sculptor José Rodrigues to create a new fountain and the result was the **Cubo** with its seven doves. It is a pity that they put it here. It is a symbol of our quest for liberty and the force of our determination deserves more open vistas. But there it stands, opposite the Almadas' fountain.

Motor vehicles now reign supreme here, but up until the turn of the century this was where the ox wagons waited for loads to be conveyed to warehouses or private homes. Meanwhile, impervious to the new image imprinted upon these squares, the **Mercado da Ribeira** has resisted all attempts to remove it from its traditional place on the river bank. The Market is an integral part of the tumble of buildings which delights the eye of the traveller arriving from the south by way of the

D. Luis I bridge. Vegetables and fruit, craftwork and fish, poultry and clothing, olives and flowers, everything is to be found in the stalls of the marketwomen. Colour and bustle, shouting and laughter, such is the backdrop to this continuous hurly-burly. Sometimes an exceptionally colourful expression may be heard in the commotion, bringing a blush to the cheeks of the more bashful young ladies; no contempt or insult is intended, it simply reflects the straightforwardness of these good and simple people, their honest lack of refinement and their direct way of calling things by the name by which they have always known them.

An endeavor is being made to restore this labyrinth of streets and old houses in an authentic style. The old houses of **Miragaia**, which could be said to be an ex-

Old houses on the Praça da Ribeira.

The market at the Ribeira.

Praça da Ribeira.

tension of the **Ribeira** on the way to the sea, are also being restored.

The whole **Barredo** district, from the Cathedral to the river, is undergoing restoration. And it is a pleasure indeed to wander in its winding streets, to find an archway of the old Suevi wall, a fountain, a small bar which, in the summer, becomes a bright cafe terrace, a greengrocer specializing in the sale of salt cod and drinks. And this pleasure is renewed on every corner of every street in the old quarters of the city — the **Sé, Vitória** and **São Nicolau.**

And each sunny day renews the joy of living — every window, every smell, on every corner. We have only to open our eyes and our ears and every interior will re-

veal itself to us as it truly is, without disguise, in the washing hanging outside the window to dry, the smell of cooking on the stove, the louder words spoken by the raised voices indoors. Their lives are revealed in the eyes and smiles of the people we encounter and is what makes us feel at home whenever we come into contact with the **Ribeira** and its people. And every modest or not so modest restaurant in the area will undoubtedly offer one or two typical Oporto dishes, a good wine (be it from the lowliest barrel or the most extravagant bottle) and the satisfaction which never palls of dispensing hospitality...to those who come in the right spirit.

An old establishment in the Cordoaria district.

Interesting sights in the Barredo and the S. Nicolau districts.

Street Café in Praça da Ribeira.

The old quarter of Miragaia.

Interior of the Church of São Francisco.

IGREJA DE S. FRANCISCO

This church is also known as the Church of Gold, so stumptuous are the gilt carvings in its genuinely Gothic interior. This church belonged to the Franciscan monastery which was established here in the XIII century, against the will of the influential Bishop Pedro Salvadores. Construction proceeded despite the difficulties which this typical example of the powerful medieval lord placed in their way and it was only in 1425, under the personal patronage of King João I, that it was completed. It has a nave and two aisles, lighted by a handsome rose window, symbol of the *Rosa Fortunae*. But the most striking feature is the baroque splendour of its gilt carvings, produced in the XVII to mid-XVIII centuries.

The monastery burnt down during the Siege of Oporto in 1832, supposedly to "roast" the liberal battalion that was quartered there. Only the original church is left, and even that has lost part of the left hand side of its facade, amputated by the **Palácio da Associação Comercial do Porto**. The **Pátio das Nações** was built on the ruins of the former monastery cloister. At dusk, the setting sun playing over the gilt carving is an unforgettable spectacle.

The beautiful Palácio da Bolsa *(Stock Exchange).*

The former Tribunal do Comércio; *the* Sala Dourada.

BOLSA

Everybody calls this building the **Palácio da Bolsa** or Stock Exchange but it was originally built in the XIX century, as the headquarters of the **Associação do Porto**. It was designed by the architect Joaquim da Costa Lima. The main entrance opens onto the **Pátio das Nações**, which was given this name in reference to the fact that the upper cornice, beneath the metallic dome, bears the arms of the nations with which the Association maintained relations. This is where the brokers from the Commodity Exchange and the Stock Exchange gathered and hence the name by which the Palace came to be known. The Oporto stock exchange continues to operate from these premises today.

When the **Associação Comercial do Porto** decided to undertake the task of building headquarters for themselves, they employed a very unusual process for raising the necessary funds for the project: they taxed themselves and thus raised the money to get the project going. Two years later, in 1836, the government allocated them the site of the former **Convento de S. Francisco** and work commenced.

The administrative services operate from the ground floor and visitors are admitted only to the first floor. The former **Tribunal do Comércio** or Commercial Court, with paintings by Veloso Salgado and furniture by José Marques da Silva, is preserved today in its original form. A small door at the end opens onto a gallery containing paintings by Henrique Medina. This artist was born in Oporto in 1901 and he presented some of his wonderful paintings to the Association to be hung here as reminders of his art and outstanding talent as a portraitist. The **Sala Dourada** contains portraits of the last monarchs of Portugal and a beautiful carved table, the work of a lowly Association employee which won a first prize in the Paris Exposition in 1869.

From here one moves on to the stately **Salão Árabe** which took 18 years to complete and was designed by Gonçalves de Sousa, based on the famous Alhambra

The Moorish Hall, *inside the Stock Exchange.*   Conference Hall *in the* Ateneu Comercial.

of Granada. It has two storeys, and contains thirty-two columns, a light and graceful ceiling, all in tones of blue and gold with touches of red and, when fully lit, it is a magnificent sight for those who have the opportunity to view it.

Not to be missed is the magnificent stairway in granite and marble, with balustrades, divided into two parallel flights, with finely carved pillars — particularly notable are the flowers in granite, which are worked in such a way that they appear to be stuck on, though they are in fact carved in the stone from which they emerge.

THE ATENEU

Culture has always had a special place in the life of Oporto and there are many institutions which, in one way or another, are devoted to this end, many of them with over a hundred years service to their credit.

These include the **Ateneu Comercial do Porto** (a descendant of the XIX century *Sociedade Nova Eu-*

terpe), with one of Oporto's most impressive private libraries, a fabulous art collection and a hall for lectures, poetry readings and the presentation of books. It has a bar, restaurant and game room and halls in which members may simply relax. Particularly noteworthy is the readiness to allow students to consult the library regardless of whether they are members.

Another organization of this kind is the **Clube Portuense** or the **Clube dos Fenianos Portuenses**. Other bodies continue to do their part to ensure that culture — which led the merchants of Oporto to have their Opera built — is kept alive, as for instance the **Teatro Experimental do Porto** and the **Seiva Trupe** as well as the novel **Associação Cultural Portuense**. In addition, there are numerous groups and associations of the local inhabitants who say that culture is not the exclusive preserve of the well-to-do. An interesting note is that the activities of one of Portugal's largest sports clubs — **Futebol Clube do Porto** — used to include a theatre section.

The Cathedral.

SÉ DO PORTO

The Cathedral, which looks like a medieval fortress, towers over the entire slope of the city that overlooks the river. In 1120, Teresa, widow of Count Henrique, bestowed the *portus* of the Douro on Bishop Hugo of the Cluny order. In 1123, the Bishop granted a charter to the inhabitants of the hill on which he was to build his church. This was constructed during the XII and XIII century and the Gothic cloister was added during the following century. Like all large places of worship, it was altered as time went by, thus losing part of its original design. Particularly extensive changes were made during the period of the *vacant see* between 1717 and 1741. The galilee was added on the north side — a porch reached by way of a narrow stairway bordered by a balustrade, attributed to the Italian Nicolau

Nasoni, with its construction date (1736) inscribed on one of the tile panels. The portico is likewise an XVIII century graft. Nothing remains of the original Romanesque doorway. Only the rose window survived, but even this is obstructed by the balcony and columns erected before it.

Inside, both the high altar and the choir stalls have been subject to change. But, even today, you still get a feeling of solidity and silence as you cross the threshold. The church is of cruciform plan, with a nave and two aisles, Romanesque-Gothic arches, granite barrel vault divided by arches emerging from columns. The chancel (XVII century, under the direction of Bishop Gonçalo Morais) is impressive indeed. The vault is of granite and marble, and carved in panels. Pilasters with gilt capitals support the triumphal arch. The splendid altarpiece of the high altar is flanked by equally impressive twisted columns.

The Cloister.

A door at the corner of the south transept leads to the late XIV century Gothic cloister decorated with XVIII century azulejos depicting the life of the Virgin and Ovid's Metamorphoses.
It was here in the Cathedral that the parents of Prince Henry the Navigator, King João I and Philippa of Lancaster, were married in 1387.

The Sacristy.

The High Altar of the Cathedral.

In the **Capela do Santíssimo Sacramento**, with a fine wrought iron screen barring public entry, stands the altar and the tabernacle, entirely in solid embossed silver, on which work was begun in 1632 and completed only in the following century. This is one of the few pieces that escaped pillage by soldiers during the Napoleonic Invasions. It is said that this only occurred thanks to an ingenious move by a sacristan to whom it occurred to cover the whole piece with a rough layer of gesso and plaster to make it appear worthless. The pulpit and the baptismal font are of marble, dating from the Renaissance period. A fine bronze high relief depicting the baptism of Christ, by the sculptor Teixeira Lopes (Senior) surmounts the baptistery.

It was here in the **Sé** that King João I married Philippa of Lancaster, whose children came to be known as the "Illustrious Generation". One of them, born here in Oporto, was Henry the Navigator.

The sacristy is a Romanesque construction of the XIII century; the present marble floor, replacing the original slate and granite, dates from the XVIII century. The majestic interior contains valuable furniture, tables and marble lavaboes, cupboards and a black wood clock, a number of paintings hanging on the walls, including the "Holy Family" which was once, although inaccurately, attributed to Raphael. Nicolau Nasoni's frescos are in urgent need of restoration.

The sacristy opens into the typically Portuguese Gothic cloister, elegant and solid, in broad arcades supporting beautiful tracery, designed by Antonio Rijarte. An old, restored stone cross stands in the centre of the patio. The cloister has also been restored. The walls of the four galleries are lined with XVIII century *azulejos*. On the upper level are five tile panels, also of the same period, depicting scenes suggested by Ovid's "Metamorphoses".

The São Bento *Station.*

ESTAÇÃO DE S. BENTO

The railroad station takes its name from the majestic **Convento de S. Bento da Avé Maria** (or **S. Bento das Freiras**, as it was popularly known), which once stood on this site. This large monastery was built during the XVI century, with the consent of King Manuel I. In 1783 it was destroyed in a huge fire, and rebuilt even more opulently in the early XIX century, to finally be demolished in 1895. Its *outeiros* (gatherings at which poetry was composed and read) were famous and the poet Almeida Garrett took part in the last one, in 1869, which, according to writers of the time, lasted three days and three nights.

In 1900, King Carlos I laid the first stone in the construction of the present building, originally designed by the architect Marques da Silva but which was later to be modified. Only on the day of inauguration was it noticed that there had been an oversight...nobody had thought to build a ticket office and waiting room. Cymas, pilasters and archivolts in granite articulate the walls, creating a framework for the tile panels, among the most outstanding in Portugal, executed by Jorge Colaço. Around the upper part of the walls, near the ceiling, runs a frieze of gilt blue with stylized corollas. Immediately beneath this is another frieze, this time multicoloured, depicting the evolution of modes of transport, up to the arrival of the first train in Oporto.

The side walls carry large panels depicting historical scenes. The front and entrance bear what are probably Jorge Colaço's best panels of *azulejos*: "Procissão de Nossa Senhora dos Remédios" from Lamego; "Romaria de S. Torcato", from Guimarães. Between the vaults are others which, though smaller, are equally beautiful: a cattle auction, a Douro water mill, a fountain of miracles, a country fair, a harvest scene, a shipment of wine and a kneeling figure fulfilling a vow.

Igreja da Lapa.

Portrait gallery of Igreja da Lapa.

IGREJA DA LAPA

Father Angelo de Sequeira of São Paulo wished to introduce Europeans to the worship of the Virgem da Lapa who was held in great veneration in Brazil. He was engaged in his missionary work in Lisbon when, at the invitation of the *Governador das Armas do Porto*, Diogo de Sousa, he came to visit Oporto. He travelled by sea which was the least tiring form of travel at the time. Thus, as he entered the Douro estuary, his eyes fell upon Monte de Germalde which he considered to be the ideal spot for building the chapel dedicated to *Nossa Senhora da Lapa*.

On 5 February, 1754, he blessed the statue that he had commissioned and the next year construction of the chapel began (today only the front wall survives) immediately behind the present church.

There was wide-spread support and equal devotion. On July 17 of the following year, the first stone of the present church was laid. An order had meanwhile been created, using the chapel, and it was the Brethren's money which financed construction of the church, though it was excessively grandiose for the slender means at their disposal, which explains why it was not completed until 1863.

King Pedro IV became so attached to this church that, in the closing stages of the siege of Oporto, in 1832, he attended mass here with great military pomp and ceremony, and it was to the **Igreja da Lapa** that he gave his heart for safekeeping, having offered it to the city of Oporto on his death, as a tribute to the loyalty that this city had shown to the liberal cause.

It lies in a crystal vessel, contained within a silver goblet which is in turn enclosed in a granite sarcophagus. Besides the Order's administrative offices and the church, there is an extensive Gallery containing portraits of chapter members and benefactors.

It was a very active church, particularly in the field of music, and it became the meeting point of the high society of Oporto who flocked there to listen to the concerts presented every Sunday by Ino Savini.

IGREJA DO CARMO

This church was built between 1756 and 1768 by the *Ordem Terceira do Carmo*, next to the Church of the Carmelite friars, which had stood on that spot since the XVI century. Today, the two churches still stand side by side.

The Order's hospital was built at a later date, between 1791 and 1801, during the days of the Almadas.

Of particular note is the exterior side wall, facing east, covered with a huge panel of tiles designed by Silvestri and painted by Carlos Branco, in 1912, depicting the bestowing of scapulars on Mount Carmel.

The three-storied facade is gracefully baroque, consisting of a single nave which contains very fine gilt carving. The statue of Sant'Ana, against the facade, was executed in Genoa and brought to Portugal in 1770.

Igreja do Carmo.

IGREJA DE SANTO ILDEFONSO

This is an XVIII century church, in late Renaissance style. It was dedicated to Archbishop Ildefonso of Toledo who lived during the VI century. It has a single nave and the facade is faced with panels of blue and white *azulejos* by Jorge Colaço. The baroque and rococo carved altarpiece is considered to bear the stamp of Nasoni's style.

PRAÇA DO INFANTE DOM HENRIQUE

The Monument to *Infante* Dom Henrique stands in the park of the same name against the backdrop of the old **Mercado Ferreira Borges**, a notable construction of iron and glass built in 1885. The statue was cast in Paris in 1899 and the monument was inaugurated the following year.

The Church of Santo Ildefonso.

The statue of Infante Dom Henrique *before the* Mercado Ferreira Borges.

Torre dos Clérigos.

Praça da Liberdade.

TORRE DOS CLÉRIGOS

Symbol of Oporto. This is a Baroque church dating from the mid-XVIII century, designed by the Italian Nicolau Nasoni and containing his tomb, as he expressly desired. The church was completed in 1749 and the tower in 1763. The belfry rises from the western end of the church, with the foundations standing directly on rock. Taking his inspiration from the Gothic-style municipal towers of his native Tuscany, Nasoni built the Tower, divided into three distinct sections, to a height of 76 metres. The composition suggests an immense bark-covered trunk, with a tall, flower-tipped stem issuing from the top section.

The whole tower adheres to this dramatic concept, with shapes and volumes predominating over decorations, in accordance with Nasoni's move toward simplification during the last years of his life, whereby surfaces were left virtually unadorned. The balcony, set with stone vases, offers a magnificent panoramic view over the city and surroundings.

PRAÇA DA LIBERDADE

It was Bishop Tomás de Almeida who made it possible for this square to open in the XVIII century, in the former **Campo das Hortas** which then belonged to the Cathedral Chapter. It was originally called **Praça Nova**, later changed to **Praça D. Pedro IV** (his equestrian statue stands in the centre of the square) and finally it was given the name it bears today. A large building, the former **Convento dos Lóios**, stands on the southern side, and was purchased last century by a Mr Cardoso with Brazilian connections. He had two daughters and, given his wealth, the girls were much sought after by all the dandies of the day, with the result that the walk before the house came to be called the **Passeio das Cardosas**, the name it still bears today. To the north, the square was extended when the former City Hall was demolished, in a project to create a great avenue which, however, came to nothing as the **Igreja da Trindade** stood in its way. Since the avenue could not be continued, it was decided to build the

Capela das Almas.

present City Hall, or **Paços do Concelho**, opposite the church. Close at hand stands the attractive statue of the popularly-named "Menina Nua" (Nude Girl) more correctly called "A Juventude" (Youth), by Henrique Moreira. The comely group nearby, called "Os Meninos Nus" (Nude Boys) is by the same sculptor.

CAPELA DAS ALMAS

The chapel stands at the junction of the Rua de Santa Catarina and the Rua de Fernandes Tomás. Its most interesting features are the large panels of *azulejos*, painted by Eduardo Leite during the early years of this century, but in the style of the Portuguese tiles of the XVIII century. This is one of the great "displays" of tiles in the city.

Various scenes are depicted, but all revolve around two main figures — St. Catherine and St. Francis of Assisi. Indeed, the most impressive in both composi-

tion and context, is one depicting St. Francis. St. Catherine appears in other panels, engaged in theological discussion and in her martyrdom; St. Francis in the presence of Pope Honorius III and another panel of St. Francis being borne aloft by angels.

Both the facade and the nave are noticeably symmetrical and severe. Four lancet arches support the stone barrel vault. Beneath the chapel is a spacious crypt which is currently closed to the public.

The patron saint's emblem and the "wheel of knives", evoking St. Catherine's torment, are visible in the coat of arms on the facade.

The *azulejo* panels were seriously in danger of being irrevocably lost. Extensive restoration was required, with the re-creation of some thirty broken tiles, as well as removal and relaying of 2,400 tiles. On 17 December, 1982, the task was completed. The total consists of 15,497 tiles, covering 360 square metres of wall, which gives some idea of the size of the task. The interior contains equally interesting though less valuable tiles, dating from the same period.

PÉROLA DA GUINÉ

This establishment, with its ornamental *azulejo* decoration, specializes in the sale of coffee, and is one of the typical establishments of XIX century Oporto. It is situated in the *Rua de Costa Cabral* (more correctly *Estrada da Cruz das Regateiras*) and when, in 1851, the government headed by this politician fell, the first thing the inhabitants of Oporto did was to pull down the stone bearing his name that marked the beginning of the street. The magnificent entrance to the old tobacconists *"A Lealdade"* stands almost opposite the *"Pérola da Guiné"*. It is handsomely framed by its iron door, a fine example of ironwork of the period. It is an often renewed pleasure to walk through the narrow streets (and likewise some of the main streets) and find many commercial and industrial establishments that still pride themselves on their azulejo facades or interiors.

Praça Dom João I.

Azulejo panel in typical XIX century establishment.

Two views of the famous Livraria Lello.

LIVRARIA LELLO

This is the most beautiful bookshop in Oporto, operating from premises in the Gothic style designed for this purpose and inaugurated in 1906. The pillars supporting the roof and gallery bear bas-reliefs depicting some of the most outstanding names in Portuguese literature. The firm was established in 1881 and has a long publishing tradition. It also possesses its own printing press. It actually goes back even further, in that it is the direct successor of the **Livraria Internacional** which belonged to Ernesto Chardron, a Frenchman who made his fortune in Oporto. He founded it in 1868, having originally been an employee in the *Livraria Moré*, which was a meeting place for the most outstanding writers of Oporto in the XIX century.
In fact, Oporto used to have a genuine tradition of

literary gatherings. During the second half of the XIX century, there was one based in the Café Rialto, which possessed a beautiful mural painted by Abel Salazar. The literary assemblies broke up when the café was sold to become the headquarters of a bank. Fortunately, the mural remains. There was another such gathering in the Livraria Tavares Martins which broke up only on the death of its owner and founder.
People are reading less and less in Portugal, but it is reassuring to find that in Oporto book shops that have been operating for 50 or 100 years are still doing business. There are a couple of antique book shops — such as *Académica* or *Oiro do Dia* whose owners' knowledge of books is as great as their love for them. And their friendliness has won them numerous clients in Portugal and abroad. They are genuine encyclopaedias of what is published and read in Oporto and of much else besides.

Rabelo *boats on the Douro.*

BARCOS RABELOS

These river crafts were used to transport the *Vinho Fino* (literally "fine wine", i.e. port) from the Douro Valley downstream to Vila Nova de Gaia. Alternatively, they carried coal from the Pejão mines to the city and, as often as not brought treats from the farms and poultry yards to the city dwellers.

It was the *rabões* and the *rabelos*, together with the *valboeiros* from Avintes or Ribeira de Abade, which principally supplied the **Ribeira** market. In the early days, there were no farms in Oporto and the small gardens used to grow camellias, roses and other flowers rather than turnips and cabbages. The farms on the river banks in central Oporto were hobbies, as opposed to serious business ventures. Agricultural Oporto — the extension of the original city — only became an integral part of the city in the XIX century.

And the *rabelo* boats gradually disappeared, sacrificed to the economic need for "faster and cheaper" means of transportation. First the train, then the tanker truck.

Recently, many of the port exporters have attempted to revive their past and gradually the river near the Gaia bank has been filled with *barcos rabelos* — almost all replicas of the original vessels, to remind people of the good old days when the fleet, with its patched black and white sails, plied "their" river in both directions under the power of sail, oars and muscle of the men who depended on these vessels for their livelihood.

The Dom Luis Bridge.

A view of the Douro from the bridge.

On the following pages:
general view of Oporto and Vila Nova de Gaia.

VILA NOVA DE GAIA

A new city stands on the opposite bank, on the site of the old Vila Nova de Gaia. It was granted a charter in 1255 by King Afonso III, to wage ''war'' against the Bishop who held sway in Oporto. When the King established a Royal Customs House in the ''Burgo Velho a Par do Porto'' (Old Town Beside Oporto), he seriously undermined the Bishop's privileges, unleashing a vehement conflict that lasted for centuries.

This is the cradle of the best-known Portuguese sculptors, including Soares dos Reis, the two Teixeira Lopes (father and son), Henrique Moreira, Sousa Caldas and Pereira da Silva.
Its ceramics industry is also of considerable importance. And, of course, the great port wine cellars — so well known throughout the world. This is also a major centre of the footwear industry.

Rabelo *boats by the harbour at Vila Nova de Gaia.*

A view of Vila Nova de Gaia and the Monastery of Serra do Pilar.

MATOSINHOS

This city, lying north of Oporto, is also quite recent. It used to be the centre of an important canning industry which is today in decline. Northern Portugal's major sea port, Leixões, is situated here, as is the airport which serves the city of Oporto and the surrounding towns and the largest exhibition hall of the north. This is the main centre of Portugal's fishing industry. The **Igreja do Senhor Bom Jesus**, better known as the **Igreja do Senhor de Matosinhos** is a typical XVIII century Baroque church. The heart of the city is also the centre of a bustling *romaria* (religious festivity) which retains all the religious and pagan features of most such events.

Vineyards in the Douro valley.

On the following pages:
Vine terraces along the Douro near Régua.

PORT — WINE

An ancient Portuguese legend relates that long ago, before beginning their journey to the sea, Portugal's three largest rivers met one night in Spain. They drank, as is only to be expected of self-respecting rivers, and each related their deeds in song to prove to their companions that they were the mightiest and that they would reach the sea first. Since night had meanwhile fallen, they decided to sleep and, when the sun rose, they would all set off for the sea. As soon as the first glimmer of dawn appeared on the horizon, the Guadiana chose the route south, pleasant and tranquil, through flat land that would ensure a calm and gentle journey. The sun was already warming the land when the Tagus awoke. He saw that the Guadiana had already set off and he rushed off to find a way to the sea between low mountain ranges and across intervening plains. Only when the sun was hot in the sky did the Douro wake up. Furious to have been duped by the other two, he rushed headlong through mountains and crags, hurling himself noisily against obstacles, forcing a way to the sea. Only when he could smell the salt air of the sea did he calm down a little, worn out by the rigours of the journey.

And it is along this course, driven between the rocks by the force of open water, that the rabelos sail up and down river, bearing their various cargos.

But what a strange family this is — rabelos, rabões and valboeiros — ladies and mistresses of these waters for so long.

Strabo, the Greek geographer, says that the Romans frequently used the Douro for "magnis scalpis", but we feel that it is unlikely that the ships that came to area of the Douro from the Mediterranean served as models. Neither do we agree with those who claim that Nilotic boats were the forefathers of the rabelos. Some seek to attribute paternity of these boats of the Douro

to the Vikings but, in fact, it was not until the XI century that the Nordic peoples established relations with the prosperous inhabitants of the Douro banks and this was very late in the day for them to have any influence on the numerous vessels that had plied the river waters for so long. Moreover, the oldest document referring to the "four-oar boats" which gives us a clear picture of the rabelos sailing the river dates from the year 1200. Bluteau's description in 1712 leaves no room for doubt: "the familiar vessels to be seen on the Douro with a large oar serving as rudder, called the espadela, with a further two pairs of oars to drive it".

An engraving dating from 1791 by the Marquis of Aguilar depicts a true rabelo, with billowing sail, mast placed well back, steering platform and heavy cargo of wine barrels.

The earliest inhabitants of the Douro banks, like their Celtic brothers, would originally only have used coracles of stretched hides which, though rudimentary, was well adapted to meeting the needs arising in their frugal way of life.

They understood currents and tides and thus could venture across the open sea from Coruña to the distant coasts of Albion. But it was at this spot that they crossed the river. With the passing of time, the lords of the land also came to be lords of the waters and weirs were created to contain the water to drive the mills, which were of course privately owned and were the only means by which the farmers could get their corn ground. The landlords fenced off "reserves" in the river within which they enjoyed exclusive fishing rights. Since only the central "corridor" of the river remained open, it became more and more difficult to sail it and the small, hide-bound boats were no longer suitable. And so imagination was brought to bear:

Harvest baskets and vineyards.

only flat bottom boats could be used on this rough river and, with the economic means at their disposal and the simple construction techniques with which they were familiar, they fashioned a vessel of very simple structure with overlapping planks, hence the similarity with the Viking drakkars.

The main priority was to provide space for cargo, and necessity — which is the mother of invention — did the rest: a tall mast that could be removed when necessary; the coqueiro or awning-covered stowage locker in the stern which was kept small; steering platform in the stern standing on two lateral supports, and the apegada from which the skipper controls the espadela or rudder oar; lateral oars and a square sail, frequently patched, so much so that there was hardly any original canvas left and, of course, beneath the apegada next to the prow board, the alminhas or patron saints of the vessel. The rabelos were the most recent sailing con-

cept, after the small valboeiros used near the city. These were usually steered by women who went on foot, with the oars crossed in front, coming down from **Valbom** or **Avintes** to Oporto. Then there were the simpler rabões which usually did not feature the apegada. However, the increase in wine production called for larger vessels which had to carry ever larger cargoes to meet demand and this frequently brought them to grief in the treacherous river waters.

When the Marquês de Pombal created the Companhia Geral da Agricultura das Vinhas do Alto Douro, in the XVIII century, the vessels were limited in size and then, during Queen Maria I's reign, steps were taken to make the river more navigable, by dynamiting some of the rocks that constituted the greatest obstacles. But progress was not to be stayed by nostalgia for the fair rabelos. First it was the railway that competed against them and, when the roads opened up, it was the trucks

The wine-cellars where Port Wine is aged in large barrels.

and, in the early 1940s, the tanker trucks made their appearance. With the problems created by the Second World War, the river again became busier and the sails of the rabelos were once more to be seen plying "their" river. But when the war ended, the rabelos were once again obliged to cede their place to the trucks and they slowly died in the "dim and vile sadness" evoked by Portugal's greatest poet of all time. The few rabelos on the east bank opposite the city serve as a pale reminder of the original vessels since none has the majesty of a real rabelo with the dozens of barrels they carried from the land of slate to the Gaia warehouses. And there is one for the benefit of tourists belonging to the Associação da Defesa do Património de Castelo de Paiva. Everybody remembers the days when the rabelo was a floating home for many, and how often, their coffin. In it they ate, slept, sailing or rowing or even towing it from the bank.

The port wine area lies upriver from **Barqueiros** — which took its name from the people working on the boats — and half way up the sides of the rugged valley through which the river forces its way.
This is the world's first demarcated wine region. The vines remain in the Douro region and here a whole arduous process is carried out, from planting the young vines to grafting and pruning, from watering to spraying, from harvesting to treading of the grapes, in order to see the terraces of flinty soil produce those 50 centimetres of vine which will "manufacture" the sweet-scented bunch of pale grapes which seem to have captured rays of sun beneath their skins, or the heavy black grape imbued with the gravity of those who know that they will produce a wine which was carried in casks in the fragile boats of the fishermen sailing along the coasts of old Albion as far back as the XIV century.

And how many were the nights back then when, running contraband salt to northern Europe, a drop of port served to bolster strength to resist the harsh climate of the frozen sea of the Bay of Biscay or the Channel.

It is this area, with its unique microclimate, that produces the wine to which the English devoted themselves so diligently that they took over the whole trade. It is even snidely said that their best known representative in the Douro — Baron James Forrester — died in Cachão da Valeira, *dragged to the bottom of the river which he knew and loved so well by the weight of the coins in the purse at his waist. The wine was brought to the Gaia warehouses in* barcos rabelos, *later replaced by the train and eventually by tanker trucks. There it is processed, blended with those nectars which are jealously guarded like the sacred treasure that was passed on with such pride and secrecy. The wine is stored in these warehouses, better known as* caves, *ideally in oak casks, and when it reaches maturity it is bottled and can then be sent wherever there are people of discerning taste.*

And since the offices were in the big city, on the other side of the river, the city was honoured by having its name given to the wine, this wine from the banks of the Douro which came to be called port, or wine from Oporto. Be it a dry white, a sweet ruby or a fine vintage, it needs no accompaniment. It can go solo. It is said that an old English gentleman, who enjoyed his tipple, had called it "bottled sunlight" and this is apt indeed.

One of the best port wine cellars in Oporto is kept by the **English Factory House** and, with good reason, no tourist can resist visiting one of the many cellars in what is today known as Gaia, whose doors are always open to welcome them and give them a taste of the famous wine.

Vintage Port in wine cellars.

63

Two views of the Douro Valley in the demarcated wine region.

DOURO VALLEY

The Douro is more than just a river. It is a region along the coast — the Douro Litoral, and it is a region along the southern border of Trás-os-Montes — the Alto Douro. And then there is the area of the Vinho do Porto *and the* Vinho de Mesa, *and the Douro Valley. The activities in the valley relating to agriculture, trade and transportation of wine, brought about changes on both banks of the river from which the valley takes its name.*

The borders of the Douro region changed with successive demarcations of the wine producing areas. The first demarcated wine region in the world was created in the XVIII century by the Marquês de Pombal when he founded the Companhia Geral de Agricultura e Vinhas do Alto Douro, *by royal decree of 10 September, 1756. This was the first time that the term* Alto Douro *replaced the previous name of* Cima Douro. *The first demarcated region covered an entire valley, beginning a little above* Resende *and ending at the Spanish border, encompassing towns such as* Peso da Régua, Vila Real, Torre de Moncorvo, Freixo-de-Espada-à-Cinta, S. João da Pesqueira *and* Vila Nova de Foz Coa. *The borders today are different but all these towns rightly and justly and by their very nature belong to the Douro Valley.*

The Portuguese poet Luis Veiga Leitão, who died recently in Brazil, described the Douro as follows: "Douro. Pequeno retalho de um mundo com montanhas que se tratam por tu, graças a uma vizinhança tão íntima que mal toleram a presença de um plaino qualquer" — *Douro, a fragment of a world with mountains on familiar terms with each other on account of*

Two views of the Douro River.

their close proximity and who have little patience for any flat land. And Miguel Torga, another great poet in the Portuguese language, said : "este rio é, no mapa da pequenez que nos coube, a unica evidência incomesurável com que podemos assombrar o mundo" — this river, on the map of the smallness that fell to us, is the only unassailable proof that we can astonish the world.

Slate and yet more slate, terraced to make use of every last square inch. The sun beats mercilessly on the soil which seems to boil, absorbing and throwing back the heat. And this energy is transmitted to the clusters of grapes on the vines growing in that unique microclimate, eventually producing a drink that is widely imitated but never equalled.

It is another world with a different beauty, to be lived intensely, from the river to the mountains, gulping the air of that harsh but sweet nature: the river, which changes with every bend, the colour of the water alternating time and again from green to blue, the sun which seems to warm like nowhere else in the world, and the anonymous and hard-working people, always struggling, every hour of every day.

To make the trip by boat — preferably a rabelo — or in the train that looks like a toy when you see it whistling by on the opposite bank, is to enter a world which has remained motionless in time. To visit a quinta or estate in the Douro is a privilege comparable to that of a king being received in the palace of his most noble subjects. Winter is freezing. In these polar temperatures, the Douro people plant, graft, prune, and spray, whereas they pick, crush and transport the fruit under a torrid heat. A grape harvest is hard, harried work. There are not enough hands. This is when the rogas *appear — men, women and even children who come down from their villages on the high plains in* Trás-os-Montes *or up from the* Beira *provinces in search of a month's hard, ill-paid work and all the grapes they can eat...when their employer's back is turned. Work begins at sunrise. The women cut the bunches and place them in small buckets which the children carry to the large harvest basket. Each high, square-mouthed basket holds 70 or 80 kilos of grapes. These baskets are precariously balanced and carried by a small handle placed about two thirds of the way up the sides. These the men carry on their backs protected by flimsy burlap sacks. Many also use a leather strap around their foreheads, allowing them to slightly reduce the weight on their arms.*

Then comes the treading of the grapes, when the wine presses are full. The men climb in, after taking off their shoes and rolling their trousers up above their knees and, with their arms around their neighbors' shoulders, they stand in two rows facing each other, waiting for the rogador*'s orders. And then begins the really arduous, monotonous work, alleviated by a drop of* aguardente *or a song accompanied by the traditional drum, triangle and accordion. The next morning they are so stiff they can hardly move and frequently their feet are a mass of cuts from the grape stems. It was always like this...Today the crushing is usually mechanical, but the grape harvest is still hard work nonetheless.*

And so the landscape of this long valley has remained unchanged through the years, where the nectar of the gods of Olympus continues to well from the slate heated by the sun and watered by the sweat of the Douro people.

Azulejo *panel at the charming station of Pinhão.*

Dusk on the Douro river near Pinhão

PINHÃO

This town lies in the agricultural heart of the demarcated Douro region, the epitome of all that is said of the Douro valley and the port wine slopes. It began to expand when the great *quintas* made their appearance on the valley terraces.

The railway station is of prime importance. Not so much the station in itself, but what its existence implies regarding the size of the wine industry. The station is decorated with twenty-four magnificent *azulejo* panels, which depict various moments in the wine-making process and related matters, such as the panel depicting "traditional Douro baskets".

This is the junction of the roads linking **Vila Real** to **Sabrosa, Alijó** to **Favaios, Régua** to **Tabuaço, Caves do Douro** to **Chanceleiros**. Buses bound for all these destinations leave from the station, which has made this town quite a hive of activity, whereas less than a hundred years ago it was a hamlet of humble labourers' and fishermen's dwellings on the river bank. What Pinhão lost in river traffic, it made for in rail freight and when wine began to be transported by road, Pinhão adapted to the new situation. What it never lost was the beauty of its lofty river vista, and the haze as of gold dust covering the waters on a summer's evening. At the close of a sunny afternoon, at that indescribable time when day has ended and night has not yet begun, then the river takes on a colour that is never forgotten by any that have the privilege of seeing it and fills the heart with a sensation of calm, of beauty, of peace, making it possible for us to continue to believe in Mankind.

Handicrafts.

The ubiquitous azulejos *in an old house.*

ARTS AND CRAFTS

Along the many roads of Portugal, it is common to see groups of women and girls — some of them very young indeed — who are not only offering their handcraft for sale, but actually working at it there on the roadside. Blankets, aprons, embroidery and laces. Laces of all kinds and in all patterns are on display. The roads are not all that they might be, almost as winding as the river, and the fact that you have to drive more slowly means that you have more time to see the marvels wrought by these agile fingers.

As you round a bend you are likely to encounter a table cloth or counterpane, quilt or lace bedspread. The traditional blue and white tiles are frequently used in the north of Portugal. Virtually every northern town or village features such tiles covering the buildings or existing as works of art in their own right.

And you can still find the basket weavers at work, or the man making straw hats and the indispensable tinkers who supply homes with oil lamps, funnels and watering cans. And, of course, the equally indispensable cooper, who either works in his own workshop or goes to the *quintas* of the Alto Douro, as does the basket weaver because, although the wine may be transported in tanker trucks, the harvest still requires baskets and there are still good *quintas* that prepare their wine in barrels of quality Portuguese wood.

VILA NOVA DE FOZ COA

This town was founded, or rather given its charter in the XIII century by King Dinis, who was thus obliged to build a castle here. But the space within the castle wall was somewhat limited, which meant that inhabitants in future years, or new-comers to the town, had to build their houses outside the wall — hence the new village, later evolving into the new town or Vila Nova. This was one of the places chosen by the Jews when King Manuel I issued his expulsion order in 1496. Some Jewish families fled from the large cities and attempted to circumvent the order, living quietly on the banks of the Coa river. Many "converted" to Christianity, and became the driving force of progress in the area which later, in the early XIX century, made them the target of savage persecution.

It is possibly the presence of these "new Christians" which explains the construction , in the XVI century, of the new parish church or *Igreja Matriz*. It has a

Gothic-manueline facade, a fine portico, the corners of which are surmounted by armillary spheres, one bearing a Cross of Christ and the other a fleur-de-lys. Two royal coats of arms flank a niche containing a fine limestone statue of *Nossa Senhora do Pranto*. The nave and aisles are illuminated by a circular window. The facade is surmounted by four Renaissance-style figures in high relief.

Altars with baroque carving, painted ceiling, and on the walls panel paintings of scenes from the Passion of Christ. On the high altar, a XVII century Madonna and Child, and a XVI century *Senhora do Rosário* on the side altar.

The granite pillory opposite the *Paços do Concelho* or town hall also dates from the XVI century. This stands at the top of four steps, with a square shaft and the upper edges of the capital decorated with a rope motif. An armillary and a fleur-de-lys adorn the top of the pillory.

The Parish Church of Vila Nova de Foz Coa.

The Minho landscape.

MINHO

The green province of Portugal. In one of her most beautiful poems, Rosalia de Castro wrote of her native Galicia: "Verde que te quiero verde" — Green I want you green.
And the green of Galicia is equally green in the Minho province. It could be said that the Minho is divided into two halves: the inland area with its soaring peaks, the continuation of those of neighbouring Galicia and Tras-os-Montes, and the coastal area, with beaches skirting the wooded, granite land, which is traversed by rivers, streams, brooks and gullies. There is water everywhere, nourishing the fertile land which bursts forth with flowers and fruits and where, every year, the cycle of Mankind is relived : birth, life, death and rebirth. Four seasons, four situations. It is green, very green, fringed by its blue Atlantic coast. There is the brownish-grey of high mountains, dividing it from neighbouring Tras-os-Montes, and the gold of clean sands forming beaches that are rarely visited, since the water here isn't exactly warm. "These are beaches for

real people'', they tell us, half laughing, half malicious. There is no room for half measures here. It is hot or it is cold. But never torrid, never freezing. The Minho people get into the sea for one of three reasons: to fish, to bathe or to gather moliço. This seaweed, which is also known here as argaço or sargaço, is laboriously harvested from the sea, and then dragged up the beach on primitive stretchers and left to dry in the sun and finally stacked. It serves as fertilizer on the fields of the small Minho landholdings.

This age-old industry is reflected in the typical costume that is still worn today by the local ''Sargaceiros da Apúlia'' — with their branquetas resembling medieval doublets, weathered legs protruding beneath. And their daily toil is reflected in their dances and songs. A festive pageant in which they are wearing the costume is not to be missed. In the reality of daily labour, men and women wade bare-legged into the sea, until the water is up to their chests, gripping their scythes to harvest the sargaço from the sea to provide their daily

A view of the town.

bread, since it will be turned into food by the soil en-
riched with this marine humus. Those who have tasted
the onions, potatoes, carrots or kale grown in the
sargaço-*fertilized earth know for a fact how good they
are.*

A cozido-à-portuguesa, rojões, papas de sarrabulho,
arrozada de marisco *or, for the better-off, a lamprey
eel or shad washed down with an excellent local green
wine, is an invitation never to be turned down. And,
on the subject of "green wine", we should point out
that green refers to the type of wine because, as colour
goes, it may be either white or red, with intermediate
tones. Recently, a Frenchman thought he had been
swindled because he had ordered green wine and they
brought him "vin rouge".*

*The spring or early summer is the best time to make
the train journey from Viana do Castelo to Valença,
with the sea and then the river on your left while the*
first mountains of inland Galicia rise on your right.
And, in between, the small fields, every one of them
cultivated — not the smallest corner of soil is wasted
here. A beautiful sight indeed.*

*Unfortunately, the landscape is being spoiled by unat-
tractive houses or "chalets" built by the emigrants in
the heart of the villages and towns of the Minho. But
this is the price the Minho has to pay for the large
remittances produced by the sweat of the brows of its
emigrant sons and daughters. You see them on the
feast day of each village's patron saint, cheerful and
laughing, ready to put their hands in their pockets to
ensure that the local celebrations are a success. And
their devotion remains unshaken. It is the faith that in
former years led people to build shrines on the peaks
of the highest mountains, the faith that leads these
people to travel the roads, if roads exist at all, to scale
the heights to render homage to "their" saint.*

AMARANTE

The city stands in the foothills of the Marão, bathed by the Tâmega river, and already looks as though it belongs to the province of Tras-os-Montes. Its name is reputed to come from *Amarantus*, a Roman centurion. During the days of the *Reconquest*, many of the men from Riba Tâmega joined King Afonso Henriques in the struggle for new lands and for the independence of Portugal.

Historical documents refer to the existence of a Roman bridge in Amarante, built during the days of Trajan, but nothing remains of it today. Other documents mention that a bridge was built during the XVII century by São Gonçalo, a Benedictine monk, a great promotor of weddings, who made good use of his visits to Italy and Palestine to learn something of architecture. It is a typically Roman bridge, of some sixty metres in length, resting on three rounded arches. A large statue of the *Senhora da Ponte* sculpted in granite stands at the half way point. The friar built his chapel at the right hand end of the bridge.

A flood during the XVIII century carried away the bridge, forcing the local population to urgently begin construction of a replacement. The new bridge was designed by Carlos Amarante, and was inaugurated in October 1778. Today, **Amarante** stands half way along the motor way which will link Oporto to Bragança — the highway for development of Tras-os-Montes in the north east — and the city is bypassed by anyone wishing to travel beyond it, meaning that the beauty of this landscape is completely lost. This is tragic, for the lingering beauty of the Minho here where it meets the foothills of the Marão provides a beautiful landscape which acquires a totally different complexion, depending whether you see it in the summer or in the winter. Men tried to tame the river, but its force during the winter has, until now, carried all before it. And it rises so high that it submerges the island to the north of the bridge.

At the Marão end, the snow continues to create new and different tones from the green of the slopes

The bridge and Convent of São Gonçalo.

The Convent and Church of São Gonçalo.

around Amarante and, at times, it even blocks the roads. The old road, between **Amarante** and **Vila Real**, was dangerously winding. And the new highway is by no means ideal for it tempts the driver to excesses of speed, but it is an improvement on its predecessor. In the heat of summer, the river becomes an ideal spot for small rowing boats and swimmers. Campers converge on the island to enjoy the Tâmega in cool comfort.

The *Convento de S. Gonçalo* was founded in 1540 by King João III and his wife, Queen Catarina. The monastery was designed by the Dominican Frei Julião Romero. The site was difficult, possibly explaining why the project took eighty years to complete, which of course deprived it of any kind of structural unity. Nonetheless, this monastery and its church are one of the major monuments of northern Portugal. Under

Spanish influence, the upper part of the facade contains two rectangular windows and a rose window. The portico is three storeys high — the top storey is baroque while the two lower levels are in the Renaissance style. Statues of S. Domingos and St. Francis of Assisi stand in niches. Granite statues of the four kings who successively sponsored the construction of the monastery — João III, Sebastião, Henrique and Filipe I — stand on the *Varanda dos Reis* or Kings Balcony with its five arches.

The dome is roofed with terracotta tiles and surmounted by a lantern-light covered with *azulejos*. Inside, the church is spacious and welcoming, consisting of a nave and aisles which are separated by six free-standing arches, emerging from pilasters with austere ionic capitals. The vault of the central nave is plastered, while

the ceilings of the side aisles are in panels of stone.
A majestic triumphal arch, flanked by a pair of
columns and surmounted by statues of St. Peter and
St. Paul, opens into the chancel. The altarpiece is of
fine gilt carving with twisted columns. There is also a
XVII century organ in gilt carving standing on mytho-
logical figures of Italian influence.
In the sacristy, which is hung with paintings dating
from the second half of the XVIII century, the most
outstanding feature is a fine XVI century Renaissance
lavabo. For many years, it also contained the famous
''Diabos de Amarante'' or Devils of Amarante, wood-
en carvings executed by the sculptor Ferreira, known
as Ferreira of the Devils. During the XIX century,
these figures came to be seen as indecent and were removed and eventually sold to an English wine mer-

chant. However, the local people never accepted this, since they said that it was as well to be on good terms with the Devil, and their opposition was such that the buyer, in an act of unparalleled generosity, donated them to the church from which they had originally come. They are now on display in the Museu de Amarante, which is today housed, along with the City Library, in the former monastery. Also to be seen here are canvases by two of the best-known local artists: Antonio Carneiro and Amadeo de Souza-Cardoso. The library is under the patronage of the greatest local poet, Teixeira de Pascoais.

On the occasion of the *romaria* to S. Gonçalo, on the first Saturday of the month of June, two traditions are observed of which the Church disapproves: for sale on the shelves of the local confectioners are sweetmeats in

The Cloister and the nave.

The ribbed vault of the Cloister.

the shape of phalluses and vaginas which the local boys and girls, and older members of the community besides, in fun and perhaps a little malice, buy to offer their admirers, or those they admire. This exchange of "gifts" was not just a token of courtship, often presented in jest, but it was also practiced by older generations from all walks of life to ensure that they would enjoy all the advantages of holy matrimony.

Observing the second tradition, women, young and old alike, go to the Saint's statue and tug the rope around his waist, and beg him, since he is the patron of matchmaking, to find them a husband. The fervour of aging spinsters is sometimes such that the saint is in danger of being toppled from his pedestal.

And, whatever the threat to our health, we cannot miss a taste of the traditional regional confectionery which is produced in Amarante by expert and devoted hands: *papos de anjo*, (with obvious similarities to the phallic articles of S. Gonçalo), *pão de ló, toucinho do ceu, doces de ovos*, and *galhofas*. And, to go with them, a "green wine" of Amarante, either white or red, of which we may well be tempted to drink a drop too much. These sweetmeats and wines of course hark back to the friars' *outeiros* when the monastery was in its heyday.

Moving on to the local dishes, the sin of gluttony is easily succumbed to when sampling a *cozido à portuguesa* or a no less appetizing *bacalhau à Custódia*. And, during the hunting season, you would give your right hand for a rabbit, a partridge or a quail prepared in the local manner. As Camões said: "better to indulge than to criticize..."

A Panoramic view of the beach and the City Hall.   The bullfight.

PÓVOA DE VARZIM

This city on the Atlantic coast is a popular summer resort. It was founded by the Roman consul Caius Varizinus, and it received its first charter in 1308 from King Dinis. It is known as the "Heart of the Costa Verde".

This is the most popular beach in northern Portugal. In summer, its population more than doubles. The climate is pleasant and invigorating. The average temperature is 20° centigrade. This beach has always been favoured by the people of inland Minho — Braga, Famalicão and Guimarães. The king exercised direct authority over the Terras da Póvoa, on account of court struggles and intrigues and it was only when King Manuel I granted it a new charter that it regained its privileges. The pillory, *Paços do Concelho, Misericordia* and the *Igreja Matriz* (stupidly demolished in 1909) date from this time.

Here the seafaring people play a leading role in the life of the community. The *"campanha"*, consisting of a group of fishermen and their boats, is effectively a moral code of mutual assistance between fishermen. Conversation with the old local fishermen reveals that they have a strong moral austerity which places greater store by their concept of "men of honour" than on judgements meted out by a court of law. A local figure who will always be remembered and whose statue overlooks the beach, is that of the famous XIX century master life saver, "O Cego do Maio".

Outstanding among the local delicacies are dishes based on seafood. Among the local arts and crafts, the traditional bobbin lace is more than just a symbol of the city: it is a genuine work of art produced by dexterous fingers manipulating the spools at uncanny speed. By way of entertainment, the bullfights in the old Portuguese style are a spectacle never to be forgotten. The town boasts a very popular and lively Casino.

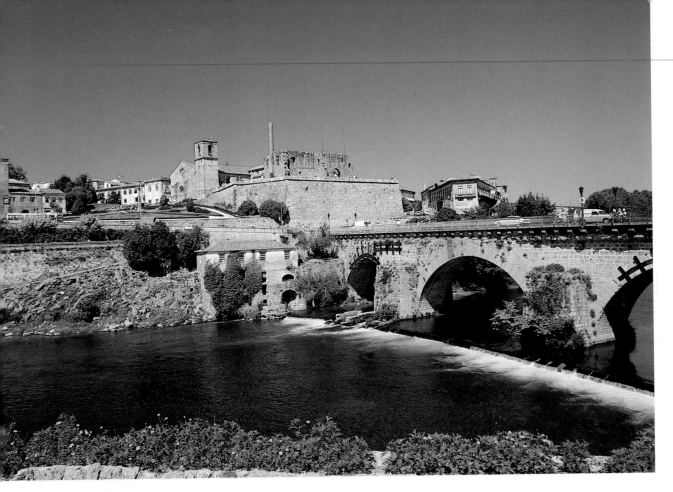

The Gothic bridge.

BARCELOS

The cockerel emblem of the *Princess of the Cávado river* is likewise a symbol of Portugal. The XVIII century legend behind this figure is very simple: Father and son were on a pilgrimage to Compostela to carry out a vow to Santiago, and they stopped at an inn near Barcelos (some say on the very spot of the *Senhor do Galo*). The inn-keeper's wife fell in love with the young man but, when she saw that she could not dissuade him from continuing on his journey, she conceived a diabolical plan to detain him: she hid some silver cutlery in his knapsack and, when father and son had set off, she denounced him to the authorities who immediately went after him and, searching his possessions, found the cutlery. The boy was condemned to death, but the father continued his journey and, after begging the saint for his intercession, he returned to Barcelos to prove his son's innocence. The judge, who wanted to finish with the affair, said that he would believe in the boy's innocence only when the roast cockerel, that he was about to eat, got up and crowed. To everybody's astonishment, the cockerel did, indeed, get up and crow. The terrified judge ran with the father to the place of execution, only to find the boy hanging from the gallows and so they assumed they had come too late. Except that Santiago was supporting the boy's feet and so he was saved, of course. This is the story behind the *Cruzeiro do Galo*, today in the **Museu Arqueológico de Barcelos,** and explains the cockerels that the ceramic makers around Barcelos continue to produce.

The town already existed prior to the birth of the Portuguese nationality, and in fact goes back to the Bronze Age. There are many Roman remains, but the oldest documentary evidence is the charter granted by the first Portuguese king, Afonso Henriques. Many possible origins of the town's name have been suggested. Some claim it comes from Barc-Caeli, a type of heavenly vessel that would ferry people across the Cávado at no charge. Others believe it comes from the word "*bacela*" which means lowland and that Barcelos means a flat, river-side area.

The town has royal origins — the charter even called it "meam villam" and in 1298 it was bestowed by King Dinis on João Afonso who was made a count in recognition of his services as chief steward and diplomat.

The successor to the throne chose to make Commander D. Nuno Álvares Pereira the 7th Count of Barcelos. However, he retained the title for only sixteen years in that, as soon as his daughter married D. Afonso, illegitimate son of King João I, the Commander immediately abdicated his titles and lands in favour of his son-in-law.

Most of the major construction work in the town, in particular the city wall, was undertaken during the sixty years that Afonso was 8th Count of Barcelos. The *Paço* or palace appears to have been begun by his son Fernando. The title of 8th Count of Barcelos was joined with that of Duke of Bragança, Count of Guimarães and later Marquis of Vila Viçosa. This was the beginning of the "House of Bragança", the Por-

A view of Barcelos.

tuguese royal family from 1640 to the end of the monarchy in 1910.

This area was also chosen by a particularly notable Jewish community, already present in documents of 1369. In the XV century, it had a synagogue, a rabbi and the Jews had their own quarter in the town. The expulsion order in 1496 led almost all Jews to "convert", and in fact very few of the Barcelos Jews actually left.

The first stone in the construction of the *Igreja da Misericórdia*, of which the remains are still to be seen today, was laid in 1593. It stood on the site of the present *Cámara Municipal* or Town Hall. Between 1713 and 1716, King João V made considerable efforts to carry out the necessary repairs and the old hospital was rebuilt.

The Order of the *Real Irmandade do Senhor do Bom Jesus da Vera Cruz de Barcelos* began construction of the church of the *Bom Jesus da Cruz* in 1705 on the ruins of a former chapel. Many of the brothers were from the coastal area, where the Bom Jesus da Cruz is held in great veneration. This order began the famous "Festas das Cruzes" — Feasts of the Crosses — in May and during Holy Week. The church, and the *Passeio das Obras*, form a fine baroque ensemble.

The parish church of **Santa Maria de Barcelos**, formerly the *Colegiada*, is likewise worthy of note. It was extensively rebuilt in the XV century, though it is in fact

The Parish Church.

The Chapel of Senhor da Cruz.

much older. The facade is XV century, but the rose window dates from the most recent restoration work in 1735 which aimed to restore the building to its original appearance. The church in fact dates from the period of Romanesque-Gothic transition. The interior consists of a nave and aisles separated by lancet arches. The light is soft, despite the fact that it filters through new stained glass windows. The walls are lined with panels of XVIII century blue and white tiles. Part of the building work undertaken during the XVI century was paid for by a former Jew, then new Christian, Gil da Costa. The sacristy still contains old wooden trunks belonging to the former Collegiate Church. The finest religious objects and vestments are only brought out on major feast days. Valuable paintings on wood hang on the walls of the chancel. The *Colegiada* was covered with azulejos, forming a "mural carpet", dating to the XVII century, part of which was reused in the sacristy. The ruins of the *Paço Condal* or Count's palace, today the **Museu Arqueológico**, stand near the Colegiada. The museum contains tomb stones and many other relics such as the famous **Cruzeiro do Galo**. The ornate octagonal XV century pillory stands in front of the church. This is a fine vantage point over the old part of the city and the medieval bridge over the Cavado river.

During the XV and XVI centuries, the main square comprised the area between the parish church and the

The Parish Church.

Town Hall which, in its present form, is the result of additions and modifications of the original Paços do Concelho. It has all the appearance of a stately home, with two towers bearing heraldic arms.

Picturesque spots in the town are the **Largo do Apoio**, the **Solar dos Câmaras**, the **Casa do Decepado de Alcácer-Quibir**, the **Casa do Baía** and the **Solar dos Pinheiros**.

Any history of Barcelos invariably mentions its Fair. It already existed in the XII century, since there are documents referring to the fact that in this area grain was weighed by the "Barcelos Measure". But the first written reference dates from 1412, when King João I, at the request of his son Afonso, Count of Barcelos, granted the town the right to hold an annual fair of a fortnight's duration, from 1 to 15 August each year. And he allowed this annual event the privilege of being tax exempt. Only the king could grant such privileges, even in lands that did not belong to him. Barcelos made the most of this concession and started holding the fair in the former **Campo do Salvador**, a site which took its designation from a chapel of the same name which was demolished during the XVII century. This evolved into the current name of **Campo da Feira**.

On account of the miraculous appearance of the Holy Cross on this spot in 1504, the Fair came to be held on the occasion of the "Festa das Cruzes" celebrated from 1 — 3 May each year. Currently, the fair is a meeting point where commodities from far and wide are on sale. The local arts and crafts are to be seen everywhere, whether at the top of the Torre da Porta Nova or in the Tourist Office, or in the streets and markets of Barcelos. These include lace, embroidery, clogs, straw and wicker baskets, troughs, articles in tin, rattles and objects in copper, weaving and rustic furniture and, especially, china and pottery. The village of Galegos, with its potters' workshops, lies a few kilometres away. There are so many that we are only afraid that we might forget some. The main workshops are: *Ti Ana Baraça*, with her typical "pig slaughter", musicians, doves and dove cots, ox carts and band stands. *Ti Domingos Mistério* with his cribs and "Last Suppers", or his three "Santos Populares": St. Anthony, St. John and St. Peter. And Julia Ramalho who produces a whole series of figures, including her "seven mortal sins" or "Holy Family". The latter is grand-daughter of the late *Ti Rosa Ramalha*, with her kings, her little girls and her Christs, particularly the Black Christ. To acquire a *Ti Rosa* piece today is a privilege reserved for the lucky few or for the well off. One might regret today not having purchased a Black Christ, a unique figure, naive but very sincere in its symbology. Júlia herself seeks to acquire all her grandmother's pieces to create a museum to honour the greatest craftswoman of Barcelos, *Ti Rosa Ramalha*.

The Cathedral.

Igreja do Pópulo.

BRAGA

This is the ancient See of a huge Spanish diocese — the archbishopric of Braga, capital of the Minho province, which is known world-wide as the Rome of Portugal, on account of its ecclesiastical importance, which was enhanced by the creation of the Pontifical Faculty of Philosophy. The local people say that something is "older than the Sé of Braga", clearing arising from these ancient origins.

During Roman times, when the city went by the name of Bracara Augusta, a temple was built, believed to have been dedicated to Isis, which was destroyed in 716 by the Arabs. The first *Count of Portucale*, Henrique of Burgundy, had a Christian church built on these ruins, which was eventually to become the present cathedral. Unfortunately, this is the country's most extensively vandalized, modified and "beautified" monument, and it is merely by chance that certain original Romanesque features have survived.

It is now a huge assemblage of buildings of which only the nave and aisles and the *Porta do Sol* are of the original Romanesque construction. The facade dates from 1727, built by D. Rodrigo de Moura Teles who, in supreme artistic ignorance, had the original towers pulled down and replaced by new ones that are totally out of character. The XVI century granite rib vault in the chancel is an interesting feature.

The imposing **Igreja do Pópulo** stands in the old *Campo da Vinha*. It was built by Archbishop Frei Agostinho de Jesus to house his tomb and dates back to 1609. The name of this church comes from that of the Virgin worshipped in the church of *Santa Maria del Pópolo*, in Rome, who was much venerated by the Archbishop. The interior of the church is panelled with XVIII century *azulejos*.

The old Augustinian friars' monastery, which later became an army headquarters, stands beside the church. The square before it contains a statue of Marshal Gomes da Costa, who led the military uprising in 1926. Other particularly interesting buildings include the XVIII century **Hospital de S. Marcos**, with the figures of the apostles on the balustrade. The XVI century **Capela dos Coimbras**, to the left of which stands the **Igreja de João Souto**, was rebuilt in the VIII century on the ruins of a Roman temple. On the other side of the road, but hidden from view, is the proto-historic **Fonte do Ídolo**. The **Palacete do Raio**, one of the city's most ornate buildings in the typical Baroque style. The **Museu de Arte Sacra** and the **Biblioteca Municipal** hold valuable treasures and deserve a visit.

At the turn of the century, the **Avenida Central** was the heart of the city where everybody met. And every nook and cranny has its beauty and history.

The Hospital and Church of São Marcos*;* Igreja da Lapa *and* Arcada Palace *on the* Avenida Central.

Pelican Fountain *in* Praça do Município *and* Capela dos Coimbras.

The church of Bom Jesus do Monte.

BOM JESUS

The beautiful rural resort and sanctuary called **Bom Jesus do Monte** lies a little over two kilometres from Braga on the western slope of the **Serra de Espinho**. It is justly renowned and visited by those eager to enjoy its dense woodlands, benign climate and wide horizons.

The Archbishop Martinho da Costa had a chapel built here in 1494. The site was uninhabited and difficult to reach and it was not until 1723 that another archbishop, Rodrigo de Moura Teles, had the monumental stairway built. A small church, which may have been round, was built in place of the chapel and was in turn demolished in 1811 to make way for the present church.

A hydraulic lift carries visitors to the summit if you feel disinclined to ascend the beautiful stairway and visit the chapels placed at the end of each landing. An interesting figure encountered is of an armed knight staring southward. This is **São Longuinhos**, and tradition would have it that girls of marriageable age who manage to walk around the statue three times in silence will find a sweetheart before the year is out.

There are some fine hotels up here on the hill top and in summer they are in great demand. A well-surfaced road allows cars to reach the very top. From Bom Jesus, you may continue to **Falperra** or Sameiro.

The Parish Church and a statue of Christ
in the Chapel of the Mareantes.

The Parish Church: a detail; the Barrosa Dolmen.

CAMINHA

The Minho river divides northen Portugal from Spain.
Santa Tecla lies on the Galician side and **Caminha**, a
stone's throw from the Coura estuary, on the Portuguese side.
Pre-Roman fortifications have been found in *Vilar de
Mouros*, near Caminha, as have other similar remains
in Alto Minho and Galicia, which suggest that prior to
the Roman occupation, Celtic-Iberian tribes had taken
refuge in these regions.
The **Barrosa dolmen**, which is perhaps one of the best
preserved megalithic monuments in Portugal, lies in
the district of Caminha, close to **Vila Praia de Âncora**.
Caminha is a charming town, centring around the ancient square, surrounded by lime trees, which prides itself on an interesting XV century fountain in the middle. The *Igreja Matriz* is a fine Gothic church which

Palace of the Dukes of Braganza and the Castle in the background.

The Castle; Palace of the Dukes of Braganza.

took seventy-five years to complete. The church is entirely in granite and its design follows that of the typical fortress-church. The side portal, facing west, is a work of high quality masonry featuring the figures of the apostles St. Peter and St.Paul and the evangelists St.Mark and St. Luke. The patron saint Maria dos Anjos appears on the pediment. The interior with its nave and aisles is exceptionally beautiful. The ceiling is entirely panelled in maple wood. Particularly notable among the fine statues in the church is that of Christ crowned with thorns.

GUIMARÃES

The city is traditionally known as the "Cradle of the Portuguese Nationality" since the first king of Portugal, Afonso Henriques, was born here. It was founded far back in time, much earlier than the period of Roman domination, as is borne out by numerous ruins of pre-Roman settlements on the crests of the hills in the region. From Roman days there remains a road which linked **Bracara Augusta** with Orense by way of the

*Another view of the Palace of the Dukes; the Church of
Nossa Senhora da Oliveira.*

Cloister of the Alberto Sampaio Museum.

Tâmega valley and the Marão. The many other vestiges of the period in the region include sacrificial altars, the Trajanic inscription, the spa ruins and milestones.

During the X century, the region was raided by Normans and Saracens and thus it became necessary to build the castle of Vimaranes. It may be assumed that the name comes from the Roman *Via Maranis*, the present Monção road. This is also why the inhabitants of Monção are called "*vimaranenses*". Count D. Henrique built his castle on the ruins of the original construction of which no written records remain, and where his son Afonso was born. After the battle at Ourique (in the course of which, legend would have it, King Afonso Henriques defeated seven Moorish kings, hence the seven castles on the Portuguese coat of arms) the king founded the **Colegiada da Igreja de Santa Maria da Oliveira**. The only Portuguese pope ever, John XXI, also known as Pedro Hispano or Pedro Julião, was prior of the *Colegiada*. But the battles continued and after the Battle at Salado — the last against the Saracens on the Iberian Peninsula — King Afonso

IV came to thank the men of Guimarães for their support and, in memory of the battle, he had a Gothic cross erected next to the **Igreja de Nossa Senhora da Oliveira**, which still stands today.

Meanwhile, the aforementioned Duke of Bragança, who was also Count and Duke of Guimarães, had his palace built here — **Paços do Duque**. During the XVI century, the Bragança family moved from Guimarães to Vila Viçosa. The palace gradually fell into ruin and it was only in 1935 that the Portuguese government had the most essential restoration work carried out. Today, the *Paço dos Duques de Bragança* is one of the national monuments of which the city is justly proud. The castle still retains its belligerent air, with a keep towering a proud twenty eight metres. Construction of this tower was ordered in 996 by the town's founder, the Countess Mumadona, after the Norman invasion. The castle was built around it during the XI century. Walking through the old quarter of the city, through the medieval alley, is to be plunged into Portuguese medieval history. There are several imposing manor houses, but that fronting *S. Frutuoso* is a particularly

The Church of Santos Passos.

fine example dating from the XV century. Houses with porches of markedly XVII century design surround the main squares and the *Toural*. There are also a number of XVIII century palaces and stately homes. There are no end of interesting details, wherever you look. The **Rua de Santa Maria** is particularly quaint.

Those travelling south out of the city must pass before the beautiful Igreja dos Passos and its equally beautiful gardens. This building, with its "Portuguese facade", dates from the reign of King João V, and is flanked by two slender baroque towers. The interior is adorned with fourteen XVIII century multicoloured French figures in paintings framed in mother-of-pearl, depicting the *Stations of the Cross*. The "Hall of Acts" contains several paintings by the French artist Roquemont who resided here for some time.

Articles of great artistic and historical worth are exhibited in the **Museu Regional de Alberto Sampaio** and in the Colegiada: the uniform worn by *João, Mestre de Avis* in the Battle of Aljubarrota; the silver gilt triptych, displayed in the centre at Christmas, which is said to have stood in the Castillian King's oratory and been left behind on the battle field; a magnificent silver Processional Cross dating from 1547, together with so many more valuable items.

The most impressive lookout point in the entire region, the **Santuario da Penha**, lies seven kilometres distant. There are at least three roads to the top, but the most picturesque is doubtless that passing by way of the old **Convento da Costa**. Besides the Sanctuary itself, there is good tourist accommodation for those seeking clean air, clean water, calm and repose. This spot lies 620 metres above sea level and features large outcrops of granite but few trees. Viewed from this angle, the city acquires new dimensions and the eye is drawn to the infinite horizons. It is not surprising that a granite promontory should contain caves. Every visit to the **Penha** serves as an excuse to rediscover them. For instance, the *"Gruta do Ermitão"* in the Summer is just the time and place to sample a red green wine during the quiet dusk of a hot day, instilling a feeling of being at one with the world.

Espigueiros *(granaries).*

The Castle and espigueiros *on the rocky platform;
a view of the Lima Valley.*

LINDOSO

As you climb the road which begins but a few kilometres from **Ponte da Barca**, climbing towards Lindoso along the flanks of the **Serra Amarela**, you enter a landscape that may justifiably be called grandiose. A rich panorama set between beautiful gorges that are 500 metres deep in places. The waters flowing since time immemorial have carved a powerful course, which was harnessed during the World War I by building a reservoir to feed the *Central Hidroeléctrica do Lindoso*. The waters of the Lima river are usually icy cold, even at the height of summer. The **Castelo de Lindoso** and surroundings lie some 200 metres above the level of the reservoir.

The origins of the castle go far back in time, and it was rebuilt by King Dinis who gave the place its name of "*Lindoso*", corruption of *lindo* meaning beautiful. It is built in a square, each side measuring 800 metres, with a fifteen-metre high keep over the castle's single entrance. It is a pity indeed that it should have fallen into ruin. From the top of the keep there is a superb view over the entire Lima valley, stretching as far as the eye can see towards Galicia.

Beside the castle is the interesting **Largo dos Espigueiros**. *Espigueiros* refers to granaries which are carved out of granite, each bearing a cross, some of them of two levels. These are the store houses of the mountain people. The Lindoso church is a Romanesque construction without ornament. It is of rare beauty and the local people are extremely proud of it and of the hammered copper salver which is used exclusively for taking up the collection during mass.

Belvedere in the Peneda-Gerês National Park.

Landscape in the Gerês; the Geira *or the Roman* ''Via Nova''.

PENEDA-GERÊS

Peneda is a large Portuguese national park which was legally recognized as such in 1971 with the intention of protecting nature, conserving wildlife and ecosystems. In truth, the park as such had always existed, recognized and protected by all who knew and loved it. A national park is not a garden or hot house, nor cage or collection of hills with a handful of wild animals. Peneda covers 70,000 hectares and constitutes a means of livelihood for the local people, as well as being a tourist resort for an intelligent type of tourism. This is one of the most beautiful parks in Europe, boasting a wealth of natural attractions.

The park contains a wide range of types of landscape: lofty mountains (among the highest peaks in Portugal), side by side with gaunt upland plains. Green-clad slopes, narrow valleys, shadowy gorges and sunny pasture lands. Altitude ranges from 200 to 1,500 metres, and a variety of flora from Mediterranean to Alpine includes the unique and fragile purple *lírio do Gerês* (Iris Boissieri), which is but one of the many wonders to be seen in this Park.

Then there is the Geira, the local name for the Roman *Via Nova* which crosses the *Serra do Gerês* to reach Astorga, from whence it continued to Rome. Some milestones have disappeared, but here there are over thirty in perfect condition. From the **Carris**, at which point the mountain range rises 1,500 metres, or from the **Pedra Bela**, the view is unforgettable, among the most breathtaking in the whole of Portugal. And the rivers crossing the park add to its beauty. As do the people and animals who live, and wish to continue living, in this beautiful region.

The medieval bridge.

The *XVII century fountain in* Praça da República; *a view of the* Rio Lima.

PONTE DE LIMA

To one side lies the *Bertiandos* plain, the romantic Lima river runs through the centre and on the other side **Ponte de Lima** is etched against the Serra Amarela. This is one of the most charming regions of northern Portugal. In the late Middle Ages, this was a small fortress surrounded by a sturdy, battlemented wall with ten towers and six gates. Unfortunately, the two handsome gates controlling traffic and the toll on the old Roman-Gothic bridge were demolished in 1875. Almost the entire wall was knocked down at the same time and only the *S. Paulo* gate and the *Cadeia* gate, both facing the river, survived.

Even deprived of its towers, this bridge is one of the most interesting in the Minho province. Part of it is Roman, dating from the days of the Emperor Augustus, and several of its twenty-four arches, of which sixteen are ogival, stand on granite cutwaters, resembling small, pointed boats.

It is also worth visiting the **Igreja Matriz** with its battlemented medieval tower, and the manueline **Paço dos Viscondes de Vila Nova de Cerveira**, the Spanish-Arabic tiles in the **Capela de Santo António dos Capuchos** and the beautiful XVII century fountain in the centre of the well-proportioned **Praça da República** on the river bank. The bridge opens onto two thoroughfares: S. João upstream and Nossa Senhora da Guia downstream. The weekly Fair is held on the broad expanse of river sands beside the **Alameda de S. João**. The cattle market is a prominent part of the *feira* which is visited by everybody living on the **Ribeira Lima**.

The uniquely beautiful avenue of towering plane trees, creating a tunnel of arching greenery running parallel to the river bank as far as the **Igreja de Nossa Senhora da Guia** is not to be missed. A special delight is apparent in every celebration, every *romaria*, every fair. In the words of the greatest local poet, António Feijó, whose bust stands in the town:

"Rindo e brincando, passam as horas
pelos outeiros do meu lugar.
— Labios risohnos tintos de amoras,
bocas vermelhas sempre a cantar..."
"Laughing and playing, the hours go by
in the outeiros *of my home town.*
— Laughing lips, blackberry-stained
red mouths forever singing..."

View of the fortified town on the Minho river.

View of the town and its walls; Capela da Misericórdia.

VALENÇA DO MINHO

Valença, which was originally a fort and is still surrounded by walls, is the first Portuguese town after Tui in Galicia. The Roman historian Titus Livius states that this area was bestowed upon war veterans who fought under the Roman Praetor Decius Brutus against the Lusitanian tribes in the area. During the period of pacification, under Emperor Claudius, the Roman road from *Bracara Augusta* to Tui ran through here (a milestone dating from the period is still to be seen). At this time, the town was called *Contrasta*, although its original name was Valença.

In 1212, it was attacked and razed to the ground by the troops of Afonso IX of Leon when he declared war on King Afonso II of Portugal. His son, Afonso III, decided to rebuild it, granting it a charter and numerous privileges, and chose to forget the name of Contrasta and return to the original Valença, which the town still carries today. Sometimes it is known as **Valença do Minho**, but this is a redundancy, although it could be said that two *Valenças* exist today: the modern version, standing at the crossroads of the highway running south from Spain, and the Monção road; and the old town, within the imposing medieval walls.

As we enter *Revelim* we encounter the beautiful *Porta Coroada* and, by way of a small isthmus, we move on to the *Porta do Meio* which carries us back to medieval days with solid cornices crowning fine houses boasting granite balconies, some with carved lintels or delicate wrought iron adorning facades and terraces.

The entire labyrinth of streets is nowadays a bustling market in which the *peseta* holds sway. The modern **Pousada**, designed by Anderson, and standing adjacent to the **Capela da Misericórdia**, blends comfortably into the ancient whole.

The town viewed from the hill of Santa Luzia.

VIANA DO CASTELO

The lines penned by Francisco Sampaio, the current head of the *Alto Minho Tourist Board*, tell us that **Viana do Castelo** is:

"Uma saudade que cheira à serra e ao mar!
A mato e a sargaço!
A este verde feroz Que nos aquece a alma
E nos prende num abraço."

"A yearning with the scent of mountain and sea
Undergrowth and sargasso!
Of that fierce green
Which warms the soul
And grasps us in an embrace."

And Pedro Homem de Mello, who wittily explains that he was born in Oporto only because his mother didn't

have time to reach home, lived and died in love with the *Alto Minho*, his manor house in *Cabanas*, ever professing his love for Viana do Castelo:

"Eu sou de Viana cidade
Eu sou de Viana que é vila
Sou de Viana e sou da aldeia
Sou do monte e sou do mar
A minha terra é Viana!"

"I am from Viana city
I am from Viana which is a town
I am from Viana and I am from a village
I am from the mountains and from the sea
My home is Viana!"

All those fortunate enough to visit the area inevitably

sing its praises. Two thousand years ago the poet Rufus Avienus called it *pulchra*. Legend would have it that the first Roman legionnaire to reach the banks of the *Lima* was so moved by what he saw that he was loath to cross the river for fear that he would forget the past, believing it to be the Letes of mythology. He was persuaded only when the centurion waded into the water brandishing his sword. He quieted his remaining doubts by stopping his ears with wax so as not to hear the sweet song that would make him forget reality.

And reality is a sight to dazzle even the most hardened city-dweller. A bucolic hillside crowned by a church of Romanesque-Byzantine inspiration, despite the fact that the local architect Ventura Terra's design was only built in the late XIX century.

Whether you ascend by car or lift — or on foot if you feel sufficiently energetic — you are plunged into a riot of green (or tones of yellow when the mimosa is blooming — there is even a festival in its honour), climbing a steep slope thickly wooded with pine, acacia and mimosa. The church forecourt offers a breath-taking view of the Lima estuary where the river sweeps into the sea. More impressive still, the view from the top of the cupola on a clear day extends as far as Oporto and the Galician town of Santa Tecla.

Continuing along the road that leads up to the church, one reaches the magnificent **Hotel de Santa Luzia** and thence to the pre-Roman ruins of the same name, vestiges of an ancient Luso-Galician castle and settlement. Here there is a stairway up to a lookout point with a sweeping vista over the Lima valley and the Atlantic ocean.

The **Basílica de Santa Luzia** is unusual, with a symmetrical floor plan in the shape of a Greek cross. Each arm of the cross has a facade, containing an immense rose window. The whole is surmounted by a huge cupola with a double lantern light.

This city, which was originally called *Viana da Foz do Lima* was founded in 1258 by King Afonso III who granted it a charter four years later. The inhabitants were fishermen and sailors and it became clear in the XIV century that the local people were much drawn to

The Basilica of Santa Luzia *and the* Lima river.

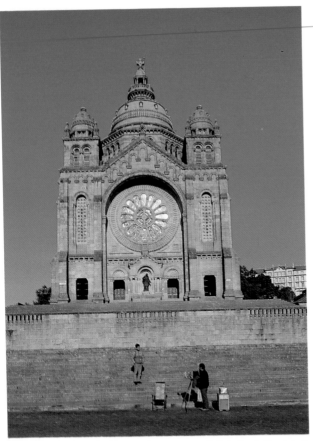

the activities of the discoveries, including such prominent names as Gonçalo Velho Cabral, Fernão Martins de Castro or João Velho. If you approach the city from the south, along the winding road and Eiffel's metal bridge, you find yourself in a river-side garden. Further north, between the river bank and the national highway, lies a tangle of pretty, markedly medieval streets and alleys, with such outstanding landmarks as the Gothic **Igreja Matriz** and beautiful houses including those belonging to the **Alpoins** or the **Melos Alvins**, the **Solar dos Cisnes** or the **Palácio dos Malheiros Reimão** and the gem of the old **Campo do Forno** and of course the *Praça* and, from 1910, the **Praça da República**. Small but typical: along one side, the XV century **Casa da Câmara** next to the **Casa da Misericordia** which dates from the same period and was designed and directed by João Lopes, nicknamed *o Moço*, who was born locally. On the west side, passing through a fine renaissance portico in granite, we enter the XVII century **Igreja da Misericordia**. A justly fa-

Facade and interior of the Basilica.

Praça da Liberdade; church of Nossa Senhora da Caridade.

Scenes of the traditional Romaria of Nossa Senhora da Agonia.

mous **XV century fountain**, carved by the locally-born sculptor João Loes, *o Velho*, stands in the centre of the square.

The *Princess of the Lima* has rightly claimed the title of *Princess of Folklore*. Anybody lucky enough to be in Viana do Castelo on 14/15 August, on the occasion of the **festas da Senhora da Agonia** is dazzled by the traditional activities, on land and on the water. Well in advance, the families living on the streets along which the procession will pass begin their unusual task of decorating the ground. With flower petals or coloured sawdust, they create endless carpets of the most varied designs and colours. They are genuine wonders which will be trodden under the feet of the entire procession following the pallets bearing the saints, especially the *Senhora da Agonia*. The Viana fishermen would not dream of allowing anybody else the honour of bearing "their" Lady on their shoulders. The procession halts at the water's edge, where the pallet is placed on the vessel chosen to carry it out to sea, followed by every type of available craft in a con-

tinuation of the procession. In unswerving faith, the onlookers in the water and on land receive the blessing of the statue which gazes lovingly at the faithful from the ship's prow.

Back on land, the procession is enhanced by the folkloric groups come from far and wide to join the procession. The women of Viana and its surroundings delve into their trunks to bring out their regional costumes, some of which have been worn by the women of the family for over a century. The housewives, washerwomen, brides...The colours constitute a living dictionary passing before the eyes of the stranger to the city; the bride in black, edged in white; the country women in red, green, or vertical coloured stripes, each proclaiming where the wearer comes from, widows in dark blue and every one of them more heavily laden with gold than a jeweller's window. Genuine fortunes in jewellery — each girl carries her dowry with her. Another highly popular event is the Portuguese style bull fight and the Viana bull ring is always sold out on bullfight day.

Views of the Trás-os-Montes landscape.

TRÁS-OS-MONTES

Trás-os-Montes *is the rectangular area between the* Marão *and the* Douro *on the border, from the Portuguese Douro to the lands of Galicia and Leon. This is a region that may, and should, be divided into two: the northern area, the highland region of mountains and upland plains with its* "nove meses de Inverno e tres de inferno" — *nine months of winter and three months of hell* — *of barren, granite outcrops, relying on agriculture and cattle farming, with a sparse population of small and medium land holdings. Second, the southern area, the Douro region, described previously. Some feel that the division should be between the Hot Lands, in the south, and the Cold Lands, in the north, but this is too facile, since these climatic variations may occur in both regions. The lofty peaks of the* Gerês-Cabreira *massif in the north, and of the* Alvão-

Marão *in the south and west inspire respect. These are barriers of mountains with peaks towering between 1,200 and 1,500 metres, cutting the coastal region off from the area beyond the mountains and blocking the passage of damp Atlantic winds to the inland areas.* **Mirandela** *marks the point of transition. The altitude here is lower, some 300 metres in the Mirandela valley, with a harsh winter climate and hot summer. Man's artificial boundary, lying to the north, is not always clear and shepherds and hunters frequently stray across into Spain without realizing it. The traveller in inland Trásos-Montes has a feeling of space and solitude. "A sea of stones...cut by natural suspicion but followed by the generous warmth of welcome. The local people are not given to the gentle customs of more southern climes. Hardened by cold or seared by heat, their na-*

ture is violent and excitable, without being quarrelsome. They are outspoken and loyal and, when their initial hostility towards any stranger who penetrates their isolation has been overcome, their natural amiability becomes apparent. There are still areas where the key is left in the door of the house until the owners go to bed, whether or not there is anybody home and a stranger knocking on the door will be told: come in, whoever you are! But beware, because the mountain dweller has an indomitable pride which demands retribution for any wrong done him. The poet Guerra Junqueiro travelled this region on foot, concluding that "while the minhoto will break a plate, the trasmontano will break a man".

This is a region of outstanding meat and sausages or enchidos (the only fish are the river trout beside which the counterpart from the fish farms pales) and the alheira which was invented by the Jews to hoodwink the Holy Inquisition. It was made of bread and poultry and hung in the smoke house in imitation of pork sausages, for the benefit of the agents of the Inquisition. Nowadays, alheira is still made in the winter, but the modern version contains pork.

And the area holds plenty of surprises: a Roman fountain that is still in use, milestones from the Roman roads, prehistoric dolmens and other remains. This is not a region to be rushed through, the visitor should take time to discover its never-to-be-forgotten sights. You just go to the beginning of the **Brinço** road and follow it southwards...

The Castle and its tall square keep dominate the town.   *The keep and the nearby* Church of Santa Maria.

BRAGANÇA

Bragança stands on the upland plain between the *Sabor* and *Fervença* rivers, in an amphitheatre, rising above the brown soil studded with gaunt rocks. It is said that *Brigancia* was founded in 906 B.C. by King Brigo, 4th King of Spain. It was a major town during the days of Roman domination and was given the name *Juliografia* by the Emperor Augustus, in honour of his uncle Julius Caesar. However, its importance was short-lived, for it was razed to the ground during the wars between the Christians and the Moors. It was rebuilt in 1130, on the site of the former *Benquerença*, belonging to the monks of the Castro de Avelãs monastery, only to be destroyed by the Arabs a second time and subsequently rebuilt. It was given its present name of **Bragança** in 1199 by King Sancho I.

People of few words, the *transmontanos* cultivate their plots with unequalled tenacity, almost magically producing a large potato patch, fields of wheat and endless "waves" of rye, interspersed with tender vegetables. A beautiful sight in autumn are the luxuriant chestnut trees, and what remains of the dense horse chestnut woods. And in the middle of it all stands Bragança which, like all historic cities, is divided between the old and the new, clustered around the **castle,** which was rebuilt in the XII century by Fernão Mendes, loyal companion of King Afonso Henriques, the first king of Portugal. The fort wall is intact and the old keep, or *Torre de Menagem* serves today as an interesting **military museum.** A pillory stands nearby which is of particular interest on account of the way in which it stands on the granite back of a *berrão* which is a type of pig or boar, in stone, which is frequently seen in this region and in neighbouring Spain. The **Igreja de Santa Maria**, also known as *Nossa Senhora do Sardão* stands opposite the *Torre de Menagem*. Adjacent to it, the intriguing "**domus Municipalis**" building which is said to have had the dual function of cistern for the fort and meeting place for the "good men" of medieval days. Outside is the **Museu Abade do Baçal** which is not to be missed.

General view of Bragança and its fortifications; portal of the Church of Santa Maria and the Domus Municipalis.

The Roman Bridge at Chaves.

CHAVES

The architect and engineer Aulus Flavius (I century) is believed to be responsible for the **Roman Bridge** which was built in the days of the Emperor Trajan, entirely in stone, "ponte lapidum", at the expense of the people of *Aquae Flaviae*. It still stands today. A pair of cylindrical inscribed pillars of great archeological value stand one on either side of the centre point of the bridge. The carriageway is 140 metres long.

All that is left of the old castle built in the XIV century by King Dinis is the **Torre de Menagem**, or keep, overlooking the entire city and surrounding countryside. The tower sides measure 12 metres and it is 28 metres high. The corners of the upper terrace project from the vertical in the form of four elegant "*mata-cães*" or stone balconies. The original town was confined within a rectangular wall, fragments of which are still visi-

ble. A walk through the old **Bairro da Madalena** or the **Bairro do Castelo** across the bridge reveals numerous points of beauty, and the XVIII century **Igreja da Madalena** in a style between renaissance and baroque is equally interesting.

Close by the old *Campo do Tabolado*, by way of an alley of plane trees, we come to a spot of utmost tranquility and freshness: this is one of the most peaceful spots in the region, of shady lawns beneath the trees, producing an atmosphere of serenity. These are the thermal springs, with a temperature of 73° centigrade, generally held to be the best alkaline water in the Iberian Peninsula. It seems that the Romans were the first to discover its therapeutic qualities, and today the water is still recommended for those suffering from liver and other complaints.

View of Chaves and its walls; the Parish Church opposite the Pillory at Chaves.

The Sanctuary of Nossa Senhora dos Remédios at Lamego.

LAMEGO

Protohistoric and Lusitanian archeological sites abound in the mountains surrounding former *Lamico* of the days of Arab domination. It could be said that there are four known "Lamegos": the ancient, the less ancient, that of the shrine and that of the sparkling wine. Nothing is known of the city in Roman days, but there are countless vestiges of Suevi, Visigoth and Arab domination. This is probably the area of Portugal that suffered most in the struggle between Christians and Moors. On account of its strategic location on the Douro river, it changed hands repeatedly over a period of four centuries.

Upon the birth of the Portuguese nationality, Egas de Moniz, the first Portuguese king's famous tutor, was placed in charge of Lamego. And tradition would have it that the first Portuguese courts were established close to Lamego, in Almacave. Lamego is rich in monuments: the XI century **Sé Catedral** with its XIII-XIV century tower, the Romanesque **Igreja de Almacave**, the **Castelo** (or what is left of it), the **Mosteiro de S. João de Tarouca**, the **Igreja do Desterro** and the **Museu Regional** in the old **Paço dos Bispos** displaying fine collections of Portuguese paintings and rich Flemish tapestries.

The stairway up to the **Santuário de Nossa Senhora dos Remédios**, rising 600 metres, originates in the *Avenida Principal*. During the XVIII century, when Nicolau Nasoni was living in Lamego where he was later to paint the ceiling of the **Sé**, he designed the monumental stairs and church as it stands today. The stairs boasts 686 steps, with landings between on which stand the **Fonte do Pelicano**, the **octagonal chapel** which was commissioned by the great reformer of Lamego, Bishop Manuel de Noronha, and the **Patio dos Reis**. The magnificent **Hotel do Parque** stands close to the shrine.

Caves da Raposeira is the company which has taken upon itself the task of selecting the grapes to produce the very typically Portuguese sparkling wine which can hold its own against its counterparts from Reims.

Praça de Camões.

VILA REAL — MATEUS

During the XII century, at the height of the Formation of the Portuguese Nationality, this was the *Terra de Panóias*, owned by the powerful *de Sousa* family. There was a settlement in the area, but only pre-Roman remains existed at the confluence of the Corgo and the *Cabril*. It would appear that King Sancho II was the originator of the idea of founding a settlement under exclusive royal control — known as *terra realenga* — in *Terra de Panóias*. However, King Afonso III took over the project and founded "his" settlement, by the name of **Vila Real** or Royal City, though the plan was not carried out until the reign of King Dinis. During the eight centuries of its existence, Vila Real has been little touched by war, with the exception of an attempted Spanish invasion in 1762 under the command of Count O'Reilly, and during the public unrest of the last century when the city witnessed numerous political events.

The **Sé** is of particular interest, established in the monastery **Igreja de São Domingos**, dating from the first decades of the XIV century. The cathedral has a nave and two aisles and a particularly notable feature is the naive naturalism of the scenes carved in the granite capitals. The **City Hall** is located in a building constructed in 1817 by the first Count of Amarante. The **Biblioteca Municipal** contains valuable works dating from the XV and XVII centuries and a large number of manuscripts, mainly of a theological nature, which originally belonged to the city's various monasteries. A national monument of incidental interest is the medieval house in which Diogo Cão, who discovered the estuary of the Zaire river, was born. A statue of the Portuguese naval officer, Carvalho Araújo, who was born here, stands at the end of the Avenue which bears his name. He died a heroic death in 1918, as Commander of a minesweeper in the waters of the Azores, after a two hour battle against a German submarine to save a merchant ship he was escorting. The **Igreja dos Clérigos** is a masterpiece of baroque art, attributed to Nasoni.

Another of the city's claims to fame are its international car and motor cycle racing circuits.

One of northern Portugal's most beautiful Palaces lies three kilometres from Vila Real in the parish of **Matéus**. It was built in the Nicolau Nasoni style during the first half of the XVIII century by the first **Morgado de Mateus**, on the ruins of a manor house that stood here previously. At the close of the century, the family heir, José Maria de Sousa Botelho, held a series of diplomatic posts in various European capitals and died in Paris in 1825. In this, his last place of residence, he promoted the publication of 250 copies of "Os Lusíadas" by Luis de Camões, containing engravings by the most outstanding artists of the period, including Fragonard.

The **Palace** is a genuine XVIII century masterpiece and represents one of the high points of baroque architecture in Portugal. The large ornamental pond in the Palace forecourt lends an atmosphere of particular tranquility and calm. Prominent on the facade is the coat of arms of the Botelhos and Morões, flanked by statues of Wisdom and Justice. The palace is open to the public and deserves a leisurely visit to gain a real insight into this great XVIII century manor house. The Chapel in fine grain granite is of undeniable beauty. **Mateus** became known the world over in recent decades on account of the "rosé" wine that bears a picture of the **Solar de Mateus** on the label of its distinctive bottle.

The Mateus Manor House.

INDEX